Alalá

Alalá

Sofía Ruvira

New York

I started writing the majority of these poems sometime around 2023. I felt for them no expectation, just the radical desire to experience and research the joy hidden behind words of languages that I now consider my own. Thank you Arteidolia Press for trusting my delirium. Thank you to Yale University and my amazing department for valuing, on the other side of the planet, something that many people are not able to value in their own land. Thank you to my family, especially to Xonxa and Margarita Fernández. Thank you Jaco, Mark, Frank, Xabi, Xurxo and all my friends who inspire me, who support me and without whom I wouldn't be doing what I do today. Thank you Zack for being my safe place. Lastly, thank you to all the people who commit the political action of speaking their mother tongue. Na Galiza en Galego.

Alalá

Cover photo collage: Sofía Ruvira

ARTEIDOLIA PRESS
New York
arteidolia.com/arteidolia-press

First Edition
Library of Congress Control Number: 2024906440
ISBN: 979-8-9889702-5-5

In Sofía Ruvira's shining poetry collection *Alalá* we witness the birth pains of words from the womb of a great young Spanish poet from Galicia, who is experiencing the eternal pressure of a young artist's life in New York City. "Just like a brick placed in the in-between of these languages", she states. In Ruvira's Canto Americano *Alalá* (Alas, in English—from the Latin *lassus*, meaning tired, weary, languid, a sense of sorrow, or a sigh of regret) she takes us on a confessional journey, moving from her post-migrant's poetic melancholia to a newly baked, more joyful Yankee's *Alas*. "My home country is Galicia, but my hometown is New York," she writes.

Ruvira's poems, written in English, and interwoven with golden threads of Galician words, occasionally morph beautifully into crafted typographic Concrete Poetry. Her New-York-School-Of-The-Moment poetic observations and journal entries are her acid etchings onto the walls of The City, where the background counts as much as the writing on the surface. I was here, she tell us, in this moment—and "we feel the hole inside her chest that un-allows [her] to breathe" when smelling petrichor in a garden after a heavy rain. Or we listen to her difficulties to say *quérote*—I love you—to Zack, the love of her life, a New York musician.

Ruvira's *palabras perdidas, palabras atopadas*—words lost and found—recall Fernando Pessoa existential utterings as well as the gesture Roland Barthes detected in Cy Twombly's struggle with words on white paper. Barthes wrote that it's not about seeing/reading Twombly's product, to think or to taste it—but about understanding the <u>movement</u> that brought it forward. We need to know about the *movemento* in order to see again, to identify, or even to enjoy it. Ruvira's poetry creates such a knowledge, where understanding takes place. At the end of the collection, she is enjoying herself in bed, reading Sylvia Plath at Coney Island and Houellebecq at Café Reggio—. She "did not come for this," but, yes, she can proudly say: "I am not a liar—I am just *eu* [me.]"

Frank Hentschker, Martin E. Segal Theatre Center
The Graduate Center CUNY, New York

en cus unen
las maneras del lenguaje

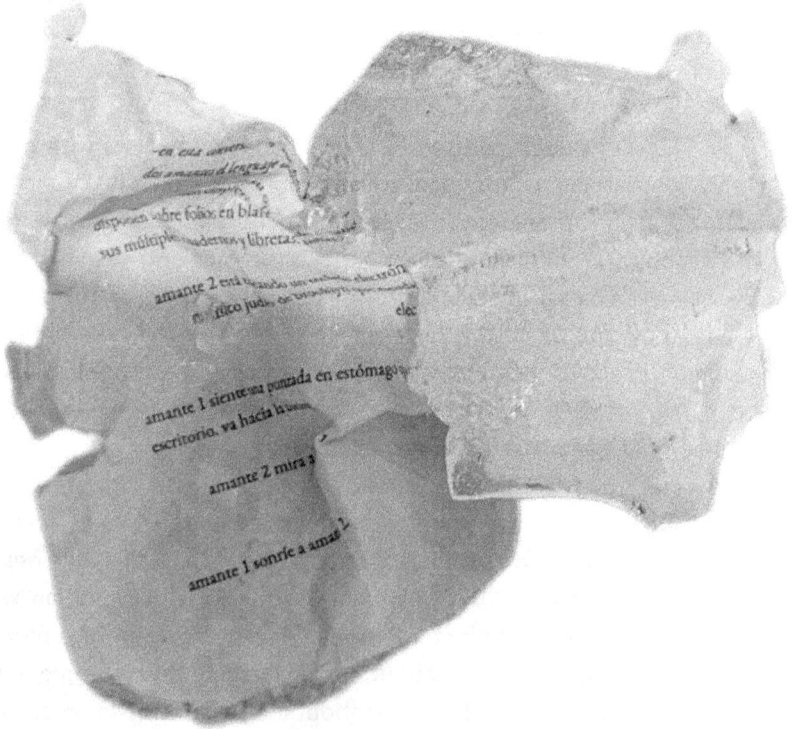

dispuestas sobre folios en blan
sus múltiples cuadernos y libretas

amante 2 en
físico jueg

amante 1 siente una puntada en estómago
escritorio, va hacia la

amante 2 mira a

amante 1 sonríe a amant

coming from afar

clouds   rising star   —   t

   there is something

      algo

     abaixo

        language spoken in the way that
                           I can

cannot express myself
 I am whimsical
      and clumsy *eu*   *son*   *dixen* *que quería*

lonxe fun   I am made of
flowers and desire
       the one who can name
                existence
I see somebody
    boarding a plane   *adeus papá* *lonxe fun*
     a language nobody understands
   from an oppressed land   not
even   recognized
I say and sing and sew and fly and glide and soar
    movemento presente feito de area   not
touching sand anymore

   at least from now on

if I trace

a line   from cross to cross I see
                                        my
abandoned self

    land
reflexo da lúa meiga sorte
    I say and sing and sew and fly and glide and soar
        eu digo e canto e coso e voo e álzome e
        érgome
    They say:
                                        where are you from?
                                where are you from?
where are you from?
                                        where are you from?

    and I wonder:
        de onde son.

I fantasize on using all the words that I don't still know
like for example

     tépeda

     morriña

     treboada

     esaxeración

     bulir

     trapalleira

I don't know the world yet I can feel

       on my throat   underneath my
tongue

                a claim a desire a
gut feeling

                  of explosion

        si eu puidera escribir de todas esas
cousas

        de todos esos xeitos

      I will be writing maybe at a reputed
journal

or a university I will be lector of   some language
but of course not mine

    sadly not mine

I fantasize writing a long poem
with turns and verses and invented phrases and

                long sentences
with adjectives

I fantasize I could say the things and love
        and read the things and love
                           i n   t h i s

foreign language
I fantasize of knowing the stress of the word
    where do I let my tongue
vibrate
                    brrrrgf
    in this foreign language

quixera ter nesta noite tódalas palabras do mundo
e facer con elas unha ponte
que me levara
de Nova York a Galicia

if I could at least tell you how deep
I feel this thorn
how encashed I have
this loneliness

being unable to express myself

quero falar e non podo
quero chorar e non podo
quero maldecir e non podo

and all the words I found for that are not
at least not

registered   I I I *eu eu eu*
son am *son* am
son am
son   am
quero chorar e non podo
I wanna cry

and I can't.

particles

suspended in the air

      my breath is a cloud
      blue

and fluffy   in the horizon

      I am

    a   thought

   a blurry piece of messy thinking

  I am a cloud a hope a thought
     a little bird tweeting

               brrrrîòíí

How wild to think that
                    I am losing myself for speaking another
language   being able to   communicate   i n
another language

            when I speak   now

        I tend to forget words

cravo   argola

                                            caixón

        taza
        moito

                        but I always remember
                            the deep words

morriña
                        lembranza
saudade

            Well, I would say

        sad
                        deep words
they bring me back   to belonging.

I said bye to my dad on a blurry, cloudy day
it made me feel good,   because
 in my land we mostly have those   days
when the sky is so whimsical
and I am so willful
that I have the courage to extend my tongue
open my wide mouth and extend
my lips and
loudly but shaky
and say
           adeus

When Raúl Támez choreographed *Migrant Mother* he thought of it as
[every mexican] heritage

When Carmen Boullosa wrote about Spanish she thought about it as
a minoritized language
        tamalcitos, tamalcitos, tamales

When I decided to professionalize my Galician language I think about it as
a way of rebellion

                language, mother language

                I long for a mother
        I long for a language

at Yale University I have an office at the Spanish and
Portuguese department
and well,
I am just   like a brick
placed in the in-between of these
two languages

I can speak both
read both
love both
and hate both

I can say *hola* or *ola*
and *te quiero* and *querote*
and I can have a salary and teach   other people to
say
I love you

at Yale University they also respect my own language
they do
they will open a seminar
I claimed
preciso unha asignatura na que se considere o galego
                    e se fale o galego
                    e se aprenda o galego
they agreed

I am just   like a bridge

my tongue is interwoven with your tongue
we don't have a proper way to communicate and
yet
we have resignified all the words

and their
meanings

you said *quérote* on a hot, humid morning of August
I said I love you for the first time

and although you   doubted if you
did love me

you were cautious
did not responded

years passed by and you say
te quiero
or *quérote*
and I still say I love you
but also *te quiero*
and *quérote*
and any of those love words
and love forms
feel legitimate
to be said
in our own way

what do you see
when you stare at me?
when you talk to me?
superfluously, I guess
my body
my white skin but my Spanish accent
I don't belong there and yet
you think I am from somewhere else   somewhere
not in America

                                              I do live here
                                     and pay my bills here
                                          and work here
                                          and study here
                                           and love here
                                            and cry here
                                         and mourn here
                                          and grow here
                                         but here is blur

what do you see
when I mispronounce words
and I write misspelling
and I talk with shame   sometimes
you see a body
that could belong to your hurtful idea of an American
body
a skin   that could belong to their hurtful idea of
skin
until I talk

and then I wonder
        if my Spanish accent is a hack
or a blessing

you asked me one time
what language would I
speak to my son in case
I would ever
have one

and I, quietly replied
my mother tongue

I keep inside of my body a colonized flesh
my skin is harassed by centuries of *desmemoria*
                                    dis—memory
a body that shifts constantly
        and   I find itself again

marcho lonxe da terra e fico lá para sempre

but a migrant body is a powerful tool
and I keep in my womb
a blade of dignity

when I walk home
        from class
after learning so many things
and pretending I know
        many things   already
I find how
architecture is just
so different
buildings are
                        just different
        there are not
tiny houses
roman bridges
stone streets
        but *rañaceos*
as my dad would call them
they are scraping the sky
and I mourn them the moon

when i walk home
        from class
I see myself as a high window
    or
as a worker   who repairs
these high windows
and I   keep wondering
whether i am closer
to that sky
        than to my own land

in my chest,
there is a feeling of
                void-ness
                b-aleiro
        I claimed for it to be filled,
        I prayed.

  mom called today
and in the incessant light
of the quivering screen
I am

                                eu son

She is not there, only her name
not even
the name I call her from
        "mamá"

I cannot pick up
        not even I
        can come up with an excuse
estaba nas aulas
non podía coller

When I do that I feel as if
                                I faint
wordless   to the womb I inhabited
for so
        so many days

The screen finally stops
and I see, again, myself.

eu son

In 1995 you are crying over your mother's lap
you are hungry, and she approaches you, softly
you don't know anything and yet you know everything
you just came from the womb
        of hers

*No ano 1996 miña nai está na cama mentres o meu pai
canta*
ondiñas veñen   ondiñas veñen
ondiñas veñen   e van
non te vaias rianxeira
que te vas a namorar

Circa 2004 you touch for the first time a saxophone
and sink your little fingers
on the buttons and out of your mouth
and the sound is terrible and you laugh
and you make everybody   laugh

No ano 2005 eu movo o corpo a través dun código
por primeira vez
plié relevé
e outras cousas
que eu agora ordeno
a outros corpos

In 2021 we see each other for the   first time
In 2021 we kiss each other for the   first time

It's the year 2040 and we are still, together
on a porch

on a place   I don't
     recognize
It's the year 2040 and there are
   some other people
   some other bodies

     they speak what we speak
     they look like we look
     they are what we are

I wish I could cry out loud

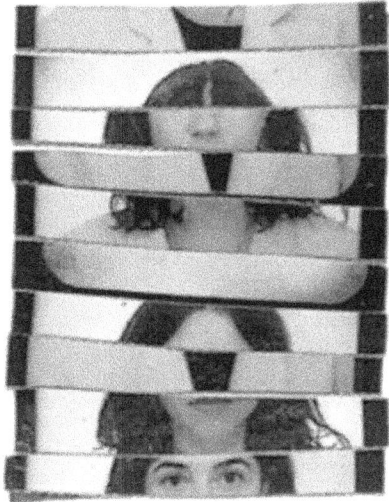

words are tight to my flesh
there is a signal
an electricity current

_____ & blood

       bhskfawdcjpisCnkjsacv sacnnca
     BJCA bcjsbcvkns c

I wait for it to be shown
    revealed

          ((((((((((glitch))))))))

there is a fiefdom
over my feet
        that others took

    [unallowed.

and now I am here
and someone is over   there
                        in the region

Lenapehóking opens up in the bright sky
the city emerges from the concrete   the dead flowers
sand
        we don't count them anymore
        and yet we yell
        for the others
        hearing;

If I must die,
If I must die,

just if,

I could hold my breath
and my arms
and my heartbeat
boom!!!

homes destroyed
the streets of Ramallah burning
boom!!!
there is a vision of the earth's splendor
there is a chant

the sky has darkened
the land was taken
boom!!!

no grass or earth or greenness
but dust asphalt flesh

they took mom
they took all of them
boom!!!

when they took up your language
        cando toman a túa lingua
there is nothing else to say
        eu podo aínda dicir
        eu son

devastation came so easy
                overnight
all of a sudden all the
flowers were gone
and we left

(.) waved goodbye at the shore;
& mom sobbed
she said
migration is not a act
It is a
        life lasting illness
she
stood still
we never see

plum trees again

my feet sunk deep in the mud
I help myself
water razed everything
I scatter in different directions
North
wind opposes
South
my face caressed

spring has come in with alluvions
      we have to build a dam
      we have to save the harvest
us
      then   *us*   *& them*

I crawl out of my bed and see   no drought
the wind yells upon my fingers
it is time

the place
where I grew up
is a womb is the earth the
place wher   p contains
myself and my   s sacred land and
regenerates the pla   grew up is a womb
is the earth the plac   up contains myself
and my ancestors   d regenerates the
place where   I   s the earth
the   place where
place wher   ains myself
and my anc   acred land and
regenerates the place
where I grew up
is a womb
earth

there is a joy I find
for us that travel   just as

      wood swallows

T: I am going to write a book.

J: A book?

T: A poetry one! Full of sentences and statements and verses and love.

J: Love? Nobody wants to hear about that anymore.

T: Why not?

J: Love is dead.

T: No, it is not. It is as alive as our speech.

J: You are so cheesy *nena. Además nosotras ni siquiera hablamo bien.*

T: I am going to write it in Spanglish. Our language *mama.* The language of love.

J: What the h*ck is that?

T: You know *mama.* This combination *que nosotras usamos.* The way we speak to each other.

J: You must have gone crazy. You don't even know how to *hablar como Dios manda* in English. You think you ain't something good for a book.

T: I am going to try *mama.*

J: Nobody is gonna want to read that.

T: *No mami.* They would. They would read me in my language. In our language. I promise.

my mom birthed me and called me Sofía

        but
        they

      our neighbors
      my high school teacher
      Danny
      my dance instructor
      the cops
      Mr. Murray
      the shopping vendor
      the waitress at Molly's

        they all call me Sophia

lovesong%

could I trace   a line that will take me from my tongue to
your tongue?
from my mouth's edge to the brink of yours

a yellow bridge, chalantly open
                                        bright

in a realm of unspoken utterances
it would have many words
and silence
like fields,   stretch and intertwine
binding our shared space
I will have access to your   echoes
and you will have access to my   inner thoughts

a line,
from my mouth's edge to the brink of yours

in a realm of unspoken utterances,
a filament of   glass,

unheard of

  They

said I duplicated someone's identity in high school

        @_____Carmen

I never knew we never knew   daddy said it was fine
        nobody will ever say bad things to me again
nobody would laugh at me again nobody would ever ever
ever insult me again   just because Dad
says it

        we celebrated   they closed the profile
roasted potatoes in the oven   popsicles they said let's
eat   let's watch TV   blurry expectation
on a brightening box   opacity

        my phone trembling   my armpits sweating
        I had pimples blossoming over my lips &   f l e s h
incarnated   What does it mean To become an Adult?
Have I ever been a Child? MadnessMadnessMadness
Republicans in West Virginia they yelled   at mom
Sudaca

We said no more and came to the city everybody   looked

alike everybody sounds alike   *que fue*   and then

                              more pimples&breast&sex

I desired   a n d

never came back

I needed to choose between writing a poem on grief

or a poem of joy

   and here I am

   counting on my tears to be spread out like a river

I came out of the my mom's womb anew

the warmest place I know to this day
her flesh covered me like in heaven
the utmost
she fed me with joy
and fresh fruits and avocados and tortillas
she sang me songs and danced me
to the sound of love
I was there but I wasn't I
I was her
we were just   us

and then   the tunnel
I heard sirens and started shuddering
and pushing
counting numbers which now I know
are so
one, two, three,
come on María
one, two...

my life unfurling
blush
...

and opacity
they took me   from

maternal cradle

our love,
living longer than we expected,
hurting harder than we wanted it
ubicuos

I promised I would buy you a house on the shore of
Maine
so you can play your clarinet
watching the waves colliding like a
        car crash

and if there is no longer a note
a sound   an accent from the diaspora
I want to hold you like the sea holds its anger

They looked at mama badly & bombed her with questions
to which she had no answer

     "pregúntale que dice" she said and I
f

       e

   l

              l

off   to the uncanny   my brain   didn't have what it
used to I did   have   no   longer

       words
I could call no *mama* but mom mommy   m y
Mother
she would say we were just

                 on vacation

     to visit the empire state building

                and shaked
when we arrived to our new home we didn't have an oven
so all we ate was cold

abrígate when the snow came for the first time and I
thought that was the end
everything remained white and that is what I imagined
when they

told us
in school   that would happen when we die
I had to go to New York City to be in communion with
God I thought
we were just
                    in Heaven

When I was younger I dreamed of nothing but becoming a popstar. I would be joyful, blissful, pretty. I would no longer be a pimpled teenager, one that has 2 friends and doesn't know how to dance. I received bad words from week to week. I dreamed of being a superstar because I wanted to make people happy when they saw me. I wanted to make my *mami* proud of myself and I would like for dad to call me sometimes. To tell me *te quiero chica*. To tell his friends that her daughter is doing something. *Tu sabe?* Everything comes down to *do something.* My brother always said he would come up with a million dollar idea. He would make money. one—o—o something in his pocket. But at that time I wasn't old enough to understand even what a million meant. I knew much, but I was not able to tell how many 0s the number has. No way.

Time passed by and he ended up working at Popeyes. I did not become a superstar. But my pimples were gone and I went to a community college where people didn't talk to me badly. They did not talk to me much, but they were kind. Mom kept housekeeping, and dad never came. Doing something, honey? Go to college, start a business. I wanted to study but was unsure if I would be able to do something with it. At home we lost our language but never lost our slang. *Sabe?* Do you want to eat *arroz con pollo? Quiere mami?* You are being rude. She was always rude. *Maleducada, oíste lo que te digo?* You gotta go outside of the hood and eat up the world. *Comerte el mundo. Vinimos acá para tener la* good life. But life was not always good. It was sometimes good and sometimes really bad.

Life was life. And it evolved as such.

I ended up doing many things. But I never *did something.*

from the solitude of my womb I write

t

h

e

s

a

d

d

est

poems

I have ever imagined I could write

Welcome to the United States of Loneliness

word

word

world

word

word

war

word

word

world

my poetry is (a) w

            e

      e

     p

       i

     n

               a pon

       g

drip, drip, drip.

       BOOM

                                        lie
lie lie lie   lie   lie
lay   down
                    on my chest

There was

inside the trains

inside the clouds

inside the eyes

inside the hands

inside the mycelium

inside the flesh

inside your ear

inside the wax

inside the blood

inside the laughter

inside the stone

sunken

encrypted

a love

I am one hundred and fifty-seven years old
I am a stratum hiding beneath the forest
of Oklahoma

I am three lustrums old
pimples on my face
a dress to buy for prom
where he will kiss me   want to sleep with me
                                      a n d
                           then

                I will bleed

I am six days old and drink my mother's milk
I sleep for two hours

                & repeat the process

I am twenty-seven years old   when
my daughter emerges from my womb
screaming
         crying

               it was the last time her father
          allowed her to do so

I am sixty years old
on a cruise in Florida while

      two planes of bullets and fire and terror are
announced

I am ninety-four years old when I breathe

                    for the last time

monologue for one artist

I set myself apart from culture

because culture is a material space

culture is not an abstract entity

culture is people with skin and legs and eyes and hands

and above all

culture is people making decisions

particular decisions in concrete places

at exact times

while you spend days glued to your email inbox

waiting for a new notification

...

a *tadaaa*

...

that never arrives

...

culture is people

with the power to say

you do

and you don't

you do

and you don't

today you do

but tomorrow you don't

and I ended up with a no

no

so many times

                    no

poetry is the last language thing I connected with

a

p

h

s   e

because of it´s   and

b

ecause I
couldn't
grasp

the form of the words
if they would   f

a

l

l

or if they were   heavy

or   light

or maybe because they would not talk to me   as
they do   hacen in Spanish

I have a Taylor Swift poster hung in my room
and yet I have never been a swifty
    I guess I just wanted to fit in
bring my 16-year-old boyfriend over
lay him down on my bed:
        "you see? I am like the other girls"
        "you are so special"

he would kiss me above a peachtree
softly   I would feel him
            &
his body
but my desire flew away
to another world
to another matter

you wake up one day

the sun is down   the light is bright

you pack your things and leave

where you go   there is still night

. airplanes. lines . passports.

goodbye to your family.   friends.   beloved ones.

yet you don't know, there is excitement in leaving

new place, sheets, new bed and pillow

a few tears which made it yours

suddenly   a   new love

it didn't take long. you searched and it showed   up

didn't mean to be there

didn't mean to be yours

a year after

maybe two

when you came back   there are two

when you go home   then is yours

you plan your life

new beginnings

                          no sorrows for land

just a body to miss

. legs. hair. eyebrows. hands.

no place to go rather than a c h e s   t

       Motherland became

                      a person

granola chunks on the floor

forgotten frisbee forgot the weed in the suitcase

papers and papers and papers and papers

a warm room

blackout and a cat beneath our bed

her hair everywhere

wet towels saxophone

      lights

airport lines

thirty dollars

four euros

love   life   trip

coming back arguments family

you inside of me I inside

of you

darkness Google weather flip flops   bread

you inside of me I inside of

you

everything gets displaced as I place myself

on the center

I came to Texas to speak

and they speak to me   they really do

and hear my words

as I speak to them   do I?

in three hours I have looked familiar to two people

in four hours three people have wondered   w h e r e   I

come from

if I don't open my mouth

maybe

I could pass as one of   these guys (?)

but I remember myself

you came here to speak

and they came here to hear my words

saturation   saturation
saturation   saturation   saturation
saturation   saturation
saturation   saturation
saturation   saturation   saturation
saturation   saturation

saturation   saturation
saturation   saturation   saturation
saturation   saturation

saturation   saturation
saturation   saturation   saturation
saturation   saturation

saturation   saturation
saturation   saturation   saturation
saturation   saturation

saturation   saturation
saturation   saturation   saturation
saturation   saturation

NO!

STOP

counting back

to   where   everything   started

3

2

1

0.7

0.4

...

forcing myself to write every day is an act of liberation

I am free as the ocean

I have a whale in my eyes

      don't cry

           she whispers

I have a snake on my throat

      he makes my voice t   r   em   b

le

          he is passionate & guilty & shameless

I have flowers on my feet

      hidden underneath my shoes

          and I don't smash them   I do not

my body is a constellation

where life incarnates

would my skin be as bright as it is

now   when I age?

looking at my palm

      I think

there must be so much more

      written inside my flesh I see

the world with old eyes

      ma ma mamá

would my womb ever hold a new being?

      would I grow?

      w o u l   d   I ?

de Austin a Nueva York

una mujer me pregunta:

vuelas por trabajo

    o vuelves a casa?

I guess—I say—I am coming home

From Austin to NYC a woman

    asks me:

are you flying for work or just

    coming home?

hogar es donde una ama

my body is a snow desert

melting

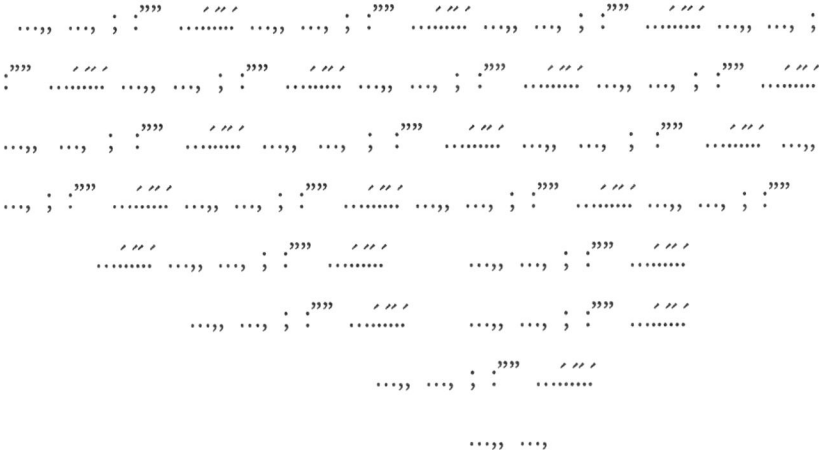

my home country is Galicia

but my hometown is New York

Galicia the place

I have been made

New York the place

I have made the things that made me

Things I Said On The Internet And I actually Like

cousas que dixen en internet e gostei

I love my legs

they take me places (home)

dance is so spiritual

there is so much strength in vulnerability

I wanted to be big

I wanted to be good

now I just want to be

I need so much water

as if my body were flowers

Moving into Lenapehóking I only carried a suitcase
I am free

                                         having green tea
                           my trachea became a waterfall

I always carry a Leonora Carrington print in my pocket
never know when you can bring somebody back into life

                    I get a hundred twenty five likes on a photo
                              and still cannot stand myself

I thought I was exhausted
it was just thirst

fell off my pointe shoes today

feeling like I am eighteen again

my body is a snow desert

wide and white

I thought I didn't belong to anywhere

until I found the place where anybody belongs

you take me to your house,

the *Critique of Pure Reason* rests

on the nightstand

as if you read it before going to sleep

because experience itself is a mode of

understanding that requires knowledge

you wear dinosaur socks

the ones you love so much

your bed smells like patchouli

which makes me a bit dizzy

you say you like to drink wine

before going to bed

and play classical music on a CD

we kiss in the glow of a candle

When I come down for breakfast at Westbeth and see the faces of those women serving oatmeal, porridge, yogurt, and hard-boiled eggs. I remember my grandmother Conchita with her arms on the table, handing me fruit while I played with my hands in a clay jar.

I think about the cultivation, about how now the butter sinks until it drowns in the pores of the bread like semen spills over two bodies that have just made love.

Morriña.[1]

---

[1] there is a hole inside my chest
that unallows me to breathe
when I smell petrichor.

CV

una curva en el extremo derecho de la costilla
un grano en el la parte oeste de la frente la
nariz suave las piernas llenas de pelo
los ojos marrones las manos finas las uñas
cortas
el pecho pequeño
los ojos grandes y marrones y las ojeras
profundas negras y abultadas
el sueño desordenado la risa floja las canillas
cortas
el páncreas inflamado la vesícula llena de
orina el ombligo con un orificio donde antes
brillaba una argolla
las pestañas largas y sucias los labios
agrietados la boca seca y a la vez humeda y
con aftas y sarro en los dientes los dientes
amarillos y anchos y reconstruidos y montados
uno encima de otro
uno encima
de otro
el mentón pronunciado la papada grande
las axilas depiladas con pelos sobresalientes
las axilas desnudas las axilas llenas de pelo

los dedos de los pies enmartillados las uñas
cortas los padrastros recortados
una marca de nacimiento en el trasero pelo
en el trasero marron el trasero y rosado y
blanco y negro y con pelo y a la vez rasurado
pelo por todas partes
pelo clandestino
un sentimiento de nostalgia en el estómago
alergia en el estómago malestar en el
estómago
las orejas con agujeros abandonados
pendientes colgando del primer agujero
las plantas de los pies sucias y planas y los
pies retorcidos y feos
mi carne rígida y a la vez flácida mis
extremidades fuertes y a la vez lánguidas
mi corazón que bombea sangre de hierba y
tierra
mi corazón un órgano entre la maleza mi
corazon mi corazon donde esta
mi corazón
mi ansia viva mi paciencia muerta mis
muñecas lánguidas mi antebrazo herido
mi espalda granulada ancha fuerte huesuda
mis clavículas salientes
una hendidura en mi maxilar una protuberancia
en mi bajo vientre
yo yo yo.

a curve on the far right of the rib a pimple on
the west side of the forehead the soft nose
legs full of hair
brown eyes delicate hands short nails
small chest
big brown eyes and deep black and swollen
dark circles
disordered sleep loose laughter short shins
inflamed pancreas gallbladder full of urine a
hole in the navel where once shone a ring
long and dirty eyelashes cracked lips dry and
yet moist with mouth sores and tartar on the
teeth yellow, wide, rebuilt teeth mounted one
on top of the other
one on top
of another
pronounced chin large double chin
shaved armpits with protruding hairs bare
armpits hairy armpits
hammered toes short nails trimmed hangnails
a birthmark on the buttocks brown hair on the
buttocks buttocks pink and white and black
and hairy yet shaved
hair everywhere
clandestine hair
a feeling of nostalgia in the stomach stomach
allergy stomach discomfort
ears with abandoned holes
earrings dangling from the first hole
dirty, flat soles and twisted, ugly feet
my flesh rigid and yet flabby my limbs strong
yet languid
my heart pumping blood of grass and earth

my heart an organ amidst the undergrowth my
heart my heart where is it
my heart
my living yearning my dead patience my limp
wrists my wounded forearm
my broad, strong, bony, granulated back
my protruding collarbones
a cleft in my jaw a bulge in my lower belly
m e m e m e

How Does It Sound To Dance In Spain?

tacutu tacutu tacututa
rarara ai agua tu cu ta tu ta tu ca
ca ca ca ca. ta cu ta cu ta x3. ta cu
ta cun sa cun sa x3. ra ra ra. vuelta
giro vuelta vuelta vuelta ole.
rarara ai agua tu cu ta tu ta tu ca
rarara ai agua tu cu ta tu ta tu ca
rarara ai agua tu cu ta tu ta tu ca.
agua. enga ahi, amo. rarara ai agua
tu cu ta tu ta tu ca. caia la gitana
ole. agua. rarrarrarra. port des bras.
fouettes.
ole
ole maria ole
ta cu ta cu ta x3. ta cu ta cun sa
cun sa x3. ra ra ra. vuelta giro vuelta
vuelta vuelta ole.
ta cu ta cu ta x3. ta cu ta cun sa
cun sa x3. ra ra ra. vuelta giro vuelta
vuelta vuelta ole.
sssssssshka. sssshkakaka. bershka
bershka shka.

ole ahi mi ninha. ole mi maria

ta cu ta cu ta x3. ta cu ta cun sa

cun sa x3. ra ra ra. vuelta giro vuelta

vuelta vuelta ole.

ta cu ta cu ta x3. ta cu ta cun sa

cun sa x3. ra ra ra. vuelta giro vuelta

vuelta vuelta ole.

ra rrra. aaiiiiiiiiiiii din din din

shshshshshsshshchchchchcccccchchhchch

chhchcc. ta cu ta cu ta x3. ta cu ta

cun sa cun sa x3. ra ra ra. vuelta

giro vuelta vuelta vuelta ole. arsa.

agua.

rrrrrarrrrrrarrra din din

ddddindondindondiiiindidndidndidndidn.

ta cu ta cu ta x3. ta cu ta cun sa

cun sa x3. ra ra ra. vuelta giro vuelta

vuelta vuelta ole.

agua.

ta cu ta cu ta x3. ta cu ta cun sa

cun sa x3. ra ra ra. vuelta giro vuelta

vuelta vuelta ole.

vuelta giro vuelta. tratra tra cua cua

cua. giro giro ole.

dun dun da dun dun da dun da dun

da dun DA.

din dun da din dun da don din da
don DA.

arsa. vuelta. fouette.

ta cu ta cu ta x3. ta cu ta cun sa
cun sa x3. ra ra ra. vuelta giro vuelta
vuelta vuelta ole.

ta cu ta cu ta x3. ta cu ta cun sa
cun sa x3. ra ra ra. vuelta giro vuelta
vuelta vuelta ole.

                           agua.

papapapapapapapapapapapapa.

                           palmas.

                           aplauso final.

a wave ends when it reaches the sea

and dies

lips cease when they meet in a kiss

and die

words end when they leave the mouth

and die

desire fades when fulfillment comes

and dies

arms falter when the embrace is lifted

-

our infinite love broke into pieces

Me, A Little Play.

Starring all the Sofías who I inhabit.

SELF: Am I alone here? Hi?

LOWER SELF: You are not, idiot (*giggles*). We are all dependent on each other.

SELF: How am I supposed to know that?

HIGHER SELF: Well, well, well. We are here, all at once. Our destiny is to be united with the divine. Or, in your case, with space. Land, Earth, your room, a shoebox. You can find your in the most absolute mundane things ever imagined!

LOWER SELF: Look, look who comes now.

LIFE: Hello, hello. How are you doing? Anything new to report?

SELF: Report?

LIFE: Inquires. Love. Food. Are you sleeping okay, honey?

HIGHER SELF: Life just gives us what we ask for.

WOMB: Tuc tuc, tuc tuc.

LIFE: I will teach you some things...

HIGHER SELF: Life lessons.

WOMB: Tuc tuc, tuc tuc.

LIFE: For example, how to fall and not hurt yourself. Now, come, take a look.

There is a CAT with the body of a hurricane that passes by. The wind he has on his toes ruffles everybody's hair. Except for LOWER SELF. LOWER SELF used hair spray this morning.

LOWER SELF: Oh, yes, and I also drank. I've got the hair of a dog.

LIFE starts to dance around, with unexpected moves, those that one might experience when riding on a rollercoaster.

To Be Continued.

[Bushwick 11 am.]

we were outside the deli

had to run a few errands

and take what we did not have

at home

you needed to get

floss, advil, coffee

the real New Yorkers

have coffee from the deli you said

the first thing when I got to the city

I did

    (you never have the real American experience

                                        until

                    you learn how to floss

                          and how to fear)

as there is a smile there is a joy

of a shared bedroom

and clean teeth

contando cara atrás lento

vexo un home sen ollos que me mira no metro

how can you hold all this loneliness

on a wagon

of a train?

                    quero

     quero   *quero*

díxen que volvería en seis meses

díxeno tantas veces e tantos meses

I am not a liar I am just

eu

Manahatta

Dead children in the
street

not come for this

Picking up a beer can

not come for this

$1100 for 20 square
meters

not come for this

Visa denied

not come for this

Zack's red eyes

not come for this

Alex touching David

not come for this

David wiping his glasses

not come for this

Screams in the middle of
class

not come for this

4.9/10

not come for this

Insufficient GPA

not come for this

90 pages of a novel

not come for this

collaboration without
retribution

not come for this

Buying a pound of
clothes

not come for this

Bruises on the knees

not come for this

Apartment without
windows

not come for this

Shirts without buttons

not come for this

Smell of gasoline, death
rattles over megaphone

not come for this

Jenna in love with Amalia

not come for this

Amalia in love with Erick

not come for this

Erick playing bass

not come for this

Concert at Mona's

not come for this

PhD without scholarship

not come for this

Traveling to New Jersey

not come for this

Kisses in Upper East Side

not come for this

Crossing paths with
Cornel West at Columbia

you did not come for this

Reading Sylvia Plath at
Coney Island

not come for this

Reading Houellebecq at
the Reggio

not come for this

Writing a book of poems

not come for this

Crying when you go to bed

not come for this

Crying when you wake up

not come for this

Regretting turning off your phone

not come for this

Brian high on molly

not come for this

Overdoses in the street

not come for this

Spending your stipend on anti-acne creams

not come for this

Masturbating every night

not come for this

Fantasizing about other lives

definitely

you did not come for this.

www.ingramcontent.com/pod-product-compliance
Lightning Source LLC
LaVergne TN
LVHW090039090426
835510LV00038B/867